Reflections

Hema Subramanian

BookLeaf
Publishing

India | USA | UK

Presentation by *BookLeaf Publishing*

Web: www.bookleafpub.com

E-mail: info@bookleafpub.com

ISBN: 9789363313873

First edition 2024

*To my Parents, Mani, Anish and Arjun, for their
unstinting love and support for whatever I do.*

ACKNOWLEDGEMENT

I thank Mani, Anish , Arjun and my dear friends for egging me on to reach my goals. There are miles to go before I sleep.

Boundary Lines

Invisible lines
Drawn around
Tread not
Impeach not
Sacred space beyond

Thoughts mine
Life mine
Repercussion mine
Not for you
To judge or state

Space mine
Breath mine
Decisions mine
Stay clear
Interference denied

Creations mine
Ideas mine
To use or throw
Breach not
Mind nor my trust!

Retaliation beware
Lash not I
Nor bash you
Silence the killer
Of your conscience within!

Alone

I stand alone
People milling around
Surrounded by friends
Yet, yet, yet, I stand alone

My conversations
With myself grows
My romances
With me alone

May be admired
For my strength
My grit and determination
Yet I and I alone

May be some touch
A hand caressing
Not for carnal deeds
But just for human love

Tender loving care
I think they call
Not for ones with
Strength within

They manage
No need for them
They are the ones
To others give their TLC

But pause
Do eyes reflect
Does smile touch
The soul within

Watch, please see
A hug, a touch
A word to appreciate
Just a hand held

May soothe and balm
The injury within
Bring a cheer
To the lonely heart seeking

Revealing Shadows

In the shadows
Of bright, brilliant days
The heart dwells
The past glory

Yet I look forward through
The shadows of time
Relishing the glory
Streaming past the gilded cage

The darkness around
Reveals the bright light
Shining at the end
Gushing fountains of hope and ideas

Determination sets in
My eyes firm and solid
The resolve sets me marching
Following the light as it beckons!!!

Colours of the mind

Colours bright
Hit the mind
Painting the canvas
With its might

Visions far and deep
Seek and grasp
Think analyse
The hues decree

The picture forms
Bit by bit
Shades merging and blending
Emerging in new light

The end result
In abstract let's you ponder
The deeper recesses
Of the artist's mind

Glimpses!

Out of the half-open window
The world goes by
Life in Mumbai rolls by
Hurry scurry of it et all

The soul of the city
Peeps at me
From dawn to night
Offering me flavours in bits

At six morn bird local flies in
From know not where
Into Arrey greens
Halting at destinations between

The reminiscence of the morning local
Mynas gossiping loudly
The crow staidly holding on to their seats
The herons sailing in peddling their wares
The sparrows chirping in unison in praise of the
almighty

Near the building gate cluster
Parents and children for the yellow bus
Gobbling cereal, some droopy, some chirpy
Huddle beady-eyed adults comparing and
contrasting

The red bus, cars big and small
Start with a trickle and then a gush
Waiting, rushing through the gaps
Finally, an impatient snail in a race

Me the constant
Sitting on my side of the bed
Watching contemplating
As the world buzzes past

Men, women, workers, interns
Flaying arms to attract the rickshaw eyes
Juggling, balancing, bags, umbrellas and things
Rushing up and down with stated stance!!

The half-constructed building
And the hovels of flats
Talks of struggles of owning
Homes in the City of Crores!

The lights in the houses
Switched on at unearthly hours of daybreak
Switched off at unspoken time to retire
Catering to young, old and the middle all the
while.

Oh! The glimpse of the Mumbai soul
From the window o mine flows
I am amazed by such variety
Sitting on my bed, I see!!

The Lone Ranger

Walk head held high
On your path assigned
Hold yourself in high esteem
Lose never your self to doubt

Keep walking down the path
Oh, Lone Ranger! As always
Born alone, you walk alone
With Wayfarers thrown in

Lone Ranger your path is of giving
Spread light and shed knowledge
Wait not for the back pat
Walk on to the next path

No one is yours
Nor are you for others
It's just the illusion
Of togetherness that blinds you thus

Walk on Lone Ranger
Newer paths you find
Take the ones that are with you
Shed the ones who need you not

Fear not, feel not
Fly free in the sky
No one to shackle you down
Walk on, oh Lone Ranger, walk on!

Seamless

Mountains oceans plains
Ponds rivers seas
Cities villages seas
All merging seamlessly

Oh! Where did it stop?
Did this country end here?
Where are the boundaries?
None visible from the sky!

What are we fighting about?
The talk of yours and mine
Is this river yours or mine
How do we divide the flowing waters?

The bulls the cows the hens
The tiger the elephant and the giraffe
Do they have passports?
Do they need visas?

Travel in and out
Of jungles across boundary lines
No controls for them exists
Yet they respect spaces of others

It's us who draw boundaries
Raise fenders to reiterate
Have checks on borderlines
The talk of yours and mine too!

The trees birds and flowers
Across lines go and grow
Why not us?
Why not us?

A Scared Heart

A heartfelt poem she wrote
Unsure of his reactions
She doesn't want to think he is to be blamed
She just wants an expression of love
Some answers to her questions
Even if they are not what she wants to hear
She wants to be happy and content inside
She awaits his understanding
Not anger or another door closed on her face
And yes, the answers
She signs off
A scared heart!!!

Happiness Meter

Percentage matters
Life giving breath
Too low leaves one gasping
Infusion courses
Instant Energy flow
Check, a timely check
Warns at times resolves

Heart beats strong
Blood shines red
Mind works sharp
With a spring in the step
Twinkling eyes and bright smiles
Check, a timely check
Spreads miles and miles of smiles

Precious Cherries

I have realised one thing,
I need to be in a happy place
and live my life to the fullest!
Do what my heart wants
try not to reason it down

My priorities have changed
My heart is stuck in its twenties
My body at times struggles
A compromise we in pact
Heart rules mainly
With rest days in between!

Age is but a number
Yet bones beg to differ
At times like these
The mind takes over control
Check that mind
Let heart hold its reins

For, the precious cherries left
Will taste so much more sweeter!!

Doors By

Shapes colours sizes
Different representations

With open arms
Welcoming all

Shutting out
The unwanted

Untold stories
Behind them

Secrets held
Within them

Myriad of emotions
Passing the threshold

Yet silent and determined
Untainted they stand!

Rejuvenation

A lil girl, chirpy, full of life
Apple of the village eye
Loved and cherished by
By young and old alike

Near the banyan tree
Green verdant fields
Dark clouds a gather
Struck the bolt on the lass

Deep wail, loud sobs
Anguished grunts
Sorrowful howls
Rented the air

Old souls in maroon
Wide circle they squat
Lay the girl amidst
Lifeless on the alter

Slowly but steadily
The grunts and chants
Raise in unison
The energy of the aged souls

Wails and sobs die
energy into rhythm sets
Slowly and steadily
Power raises to a crescendo

Incessantly flows
The power of life
Palpable energy
Of life

A faint stirring
Air intense
The sounds in unison
Now almost like one

A flicker of the hand
A gasp, a deep intake
Whispers fly
Energies retrace

The maroons breath deep
Smile hovering
Crowd cheers
With life refreshed

Highs and lows

Memories rush you back
Pulling from the archive racks
Some sweet, some bitter
Some you just don't want to dwell on
For sure, just smile and ride on

As a child, innocent, want to be wanted
The everyday affair of playing with friends to
heart's content
Mind timid, not yet strong
When, to tease, friends run away, heart broken
But then, smile and ride on

In teens, trust love and loyalty
Friends be all and end all of existence
Blind love, broken and shattered
A long time to heal it takes
Then... just smile and ride on

Life goes on with its twists and turns
Loved ones sometimes fling words
Some can't stand how harmony prevails
Spoke in the wheels to break a sacred bond
And then, just smile and ride on!

A blow to your just being
Hard hit, living becomes pure hell
Bound tied and hammered to heal
The trip mind and body need to traverse never
reveal
Hop on, just smile and ride on

On a difficult turn of the journey
When physical, mental hurl towards
A bottomless pit, one you trust
With all your heart, deals the mightiest blow
Oh ho ho, just you smile and ride on

All questioned, your judgement
Sanity, what true what false,
At forkhead, you be – cry
Integrity, in turn, of yours tested
Do you still want to, just smile and ride on?

Oh the wonder in me
Resilient as a rod of steel
Patience please hold it says
Sand and gold people will sieve
You... just smile and ride on!!!

The Storm

I float above
I see, I hear, I feel the rage
The swirling, the sucking
But is below me
Way below

I float above
I feel the pull, the tear through
The heart and the soul
But it's below me
Way below

I float above
I sense the force, the pull
To the core, I swirl
I twirl senseless
Battered and beaten
Right in the eye

I float again
Frayed and tattered
Dead of spirit and spunk
I rise slowly
Divinity in me
Spread my wings and fly!

Grief

Grief is but a loss
Of wonderful moments lost
The touch, the feel
The look, the smell
Lost, gone forever!

Grief is to look behind
Searching for the one lost
The footstep, the gaze
The sense of one loved
Lost, gone forever!

Grief is the longing
To spend some time again
The laughter, the smile
The eye messages exchanged
Lost, gone forever

Grief is but the coping
To live life again
Holding cherishing
Reminiscing the loved moments
Forever, etched in your soul!!

The Strike of a Flame

Looks, so benign
A stick and a mop of brown
Yet, the power wielded
Stands unmatched

Tons of happiness
When lite the candle, cake atop
Yet, a deep sorrow sensed
The same candle lit for vigil

A strike of match
Serves food on the plate
Yet, the same strike
A felony, burns down a barn

The bonfire spreading warmth
Lit but just the little stick
Yet, can leave you cold
The prospects of dark deeds done

Many a million deeds possible
Bringing in hues of emotions
Yet, it's who and why a matchstick struck
Decides the fate of life around!

Grasshopper Capers

I sit on a rock
on a rock, I sit
pondering, enjoying
soaking in the surrounding

A giggle and laugh
too loud for my thoughts
huge feet trampling grass
stood I still on my stately rock

praying this terror might pass
trundled along yet another mass
froze I to my spot
the colossal, me had sighted

my heart raced as thoughts paced
my end, crushed, used, thrown!
and I saw the contraption
straight at me was pointed

Oh! the angle dance kind
my mother's words, a capture but different
followed her advice did I
stood still till action subside

Unmoving, I posed and preened
Unknowing of the fame garnered
For, more shall follow
Chasing the nature's dream

Humourous Tongues!

There is a nerve missing
Tongues wag without
The violence it lashed
Watch us in delight
The screaming matches
Fans flowing countless
The protagonist
Stands naked, shredded
Under the guise of humour
The sword of the tongue at work

Smile

The gurgle, the gleam
Delights, one's heart
The instant light up,
Beaming with love.
You know, the baby,
Just loves you so.

The mother awaits the bell,
A spill of screams, chatter and pell-mell
In the crowd of delightful smiling faces
She finds the one; her heart melts
All the weariness in that instant drains
Dissolving into that one bright grin

Bright and early morning
Chirpy and upbeat the mood
The smile lingering spread
The lift man, the guard, the flower lady,
The valet, the receptionist and all the people in
between.
The warmth spreading through the miles

The warmth in their eyes
as they see you smile
the pride on their faces
as you grow and walk miles
But then, as life progresses
all that remains is the memory of that beautiful
smile.

Sunset flames the skies
Like the lover bidding goodbye.
Knowing the darkness of parting envelopes,
pasting shadows and all things bright,
Yet to take leave of his love with a blazing smile
he sinks, smiling, at the horizon, by and by.

Dawn radiantly smiles bright
Waking up the world to fresh light
brisk and bright, all faces shine
a new start, a new beginning
refreshed blood coursing through the veins
Smiles can vanquish any dull day.

An Ode to A Lotus

You lie with filth around
The stench, unbearable
But You know you are for happiness
To spread joy and colour
In the muddle!

You smile, You bloom
You sway, You float
Attract attention
To the lowly places
Thus too blossoms your happiness!!

And wonder of wonders
A nation cherishes
Mother goddess relaxes
Freshness thy name
Hope to the downtrodden
And truly celestial are you!!!

An Ode to Friendship!

Friendship is climbing the hill together
On trust and belief in one another
Laughing guiding holding nudging higher
Turning around promising better plains
Halting sharing pondering arguing pushing
Caring checking the path and sights to share
Revelling rejoicing the heights of conquered fun
Resting and gathering to celebrate in the
silhouette of togetherness!!!

Anguish and despair!!!

I try and think not
But my heart cries out
Just like our Son
Just like our Daughters
Just like our Babies
Tender heart yet

Young and vivacious
Loyal and trusting
Bought up with
Utmost care
Smallest of hurt
Anguishing moms heart

To face a day
When a stranger
Ripped the precious apart
Oh god, oh god
I stand out

Helpless wringing
Withering praying
Nothing in the world
Could I do to
Protect the tender soul
Whom I nurtured so

From the time
My womb it made home
Oh oh oh
How how how
To live my life
Still with this
Anguish and grief!!!!

So many questions
No answers found
How did some souls
Get so twisted
So as to punish
For not following
Their life their way

But beware twisted or not
you do have
To answer not God
But the mother
Whose soul you
Ripped apart
For many lives to come
For many lives to come

(Thoughts after the tragic incident in Bangladesh
where a friend's daughter was killed in a
terrorist attack)

Childhood

What is childhood?
the innate curiosity?
a fresh look at the world
discovering something new
the awe that accompanies it!
the freedom, the unrestrained happiness!!

when does childhood end?
when you are 10? 15? 20???
how does it end?
what makes it go away?
who asks you to grow up?
Does it really leave you?

WELL! childhood never ends
the innate curiosity intact
discovering something new stays
A fresh look at the world
the awe, the freedom, the unrestrained happiness
is just but an attitude! just an attitude

Childhood in 40's and 50's
is at its best
one knows the pitfalls
One knows the slides
yet you can choose to have the wonder alive
to use fresh glasses
to live life

Childhood in 60's and 70's
maybe the knee creaks
the bladder leaks
but you live life
through the eyes of lil ones
once over
keep the wonder alive
live life till you die.

The Mask

The beaming smile
The warm demeanour
But wait, strange
Reflect not the eyes

A picture painted outside
A different script inside
Venomous payback??
Reflect not the eyes

Stoic elegance epitomised
Sun-kissed blessed?
Storms that rage inside
Reflect not the eyes

Painted Face Painted Mind
Conceal the will behind
Masks of varied variety
At times...
Reflect the pain in the eyes

Baffling Tiles

Off on a morning stroll
Oh! The sight to behold
Surprise! Mind all aflame,
With something totally lame.

To be besotted
By Jove! Tiles that are slotted.
Glossy tiles
Zazzy tiles
Matted tiles
Porous tiles
Tiles my dear
Of all hues and textures

Something unimaginable
Fascinated by so unmagical
Tiles! Tiles! Tiles!
Chipped tiles
Cracked tiles
Shattered tiles
Weathered tiles
Tiles my dear
Withering in different stages

Something unfathomable
To find excitable
Tiles! Dear God
What else!
Square tiles
Round tiles
Hexagonal tiles
Pentagonal tiles
Tiles! My dear
Of shapes and sizes that differ

Pillars of Faith

Draped in different hues
Decorated and tall
In a row on display

Some born into
Some choose
By falling for the beauty of the pillar

Slowly, born or chosen
The belief grows tall
And stronger it gets as life treads on

At times, when life plays a trick
It stands tall for you to lean on
Unwavering you hold to sail through!

Steady and strong
They stand rooted in belief of one power
Unwavering of the almighty!

Toeing the Line!

Dressed in pink white and blue
Fresh with ideas too
Out in the world to play
To roam to explore
Oh the beauty, the secrets hidden unravel

Hold on says a school of thought
Wild untamed, you stray not
The path is set and tried
Unknown zones you tread not
Dangers you know not

Thus they stand all alike
Ram rod straight, unbending
Though dressed differently
Waiting to release their expressions
Trapped in the fear of the unknown!!!

The Castle

Tall standeth silent observing
The castle on a hill calm

Well guarded by the sentinels
Unwavering in their duty stand

The cannons drawn and ready
To protect and defend

Realms of history speaks
Nook, corners and the mighty walls

Of stories where the
Shame and glory of defeat and conquer

Of Prince and Princesses
Kings, Queens and Emperors

Their rise to fame and
The fall of the mighty ones!

Aeons gone by and you stand
On the cold stones

Listening to an Impassionate narration
The real lives
of the people who lived within!

The Wise and Stunted

(The Banyan Bonsai)

You stand silent as a sentinel
Watching the world go to knell
The folds tell the age you spent
Standing tired, weary and bent

You have seen the ages go by
Lives born and lost by and by
The fools you could not tell
With silence, you bore the fear to dwell

Many of your brethren slashed and killed
No rhyme nor reason to be cruelly felled
Just to satisfy their selfish needs
Brought down the mighty and weak indeed!

Is it karma turning its head around
For what comes always goes around
People felled down blown down
indiscriminately
To prove a point, nay to satisfy selfish gains
definitely

Beware, oh, the human race
I have watched time and its pace
Slow down! Balance you conserve!
For trust me and know there is not much in
reserve!!!

Ode to odes

Oh, the thoughts
And feelings
About mundane and valuable
Things around

The things that
Impacted you
Impressed you
Or sometimes annoyed you

It can be a comb
A lemon, a mom
A worker or just a thing
An object or a project!

Freely, easily
Fearlessly state
The thoughts
That fleet your mind

Pen down an ode
And walk down the road
Poetically expressing
Random thoughts galore!!!

The Parasites

Inch by inch
Metre by metre
Moved the tribe
As they quickly multiply

First the caves
Then the trees
The land beneath
Water too invaded

No care nor concern
Of the existing lives
Land air or water
All pushed over

Sucking dry the giver
Feeding off the creator
Plants animals alike
Ruthlessly vanquishing

Claiming to be superior
Nothing but a parasite
Capturing others spaces
Humans ruling the world

Musings of a Poet

My head is in a muddle
Figuring out a puddle
The poet is on a snooze
Yet the poses do amuse

A thought the poet gives
Just after the puzzled mix
The brain clicking up talk
Viewing the beauty at work!!

Tranquility

The vision of calm
Sooting coolness
Engulfs you

Yet the tiny bubbles
Pop up
Bursting the surface

Appearance remains
Ignoring the bubbles
Reigning peace

Military fatigues

Discipline the mind
Discipline the body
Camouflage the turmoil
Blend and merge in
Time your self
With silence and patience
Emerge, you will
Right time when arrives
Reveal your strength then
Stride forward reinforced
And conquer the world afresh!

Cheerful Hue

Red is the colour
To bring cheer
Know not why it spells danger
Colour of life-giver blood is it?

To stand out
To send cheer
To brighten the mood
To red we always turn to

The sunlight shines
Highlighting the hue
The glitter of Christmas
Sets the eyes a glinting

Even when tied down
Add sparkle and gleam
Bring in the festive cheer
With dashes of red in you!!!

Windows By

Windows to the world
That sees all
The good, the bad, the ugly

Peep in not easy though
Shutters at will drawn
A glimpse might lead you to depths

Yet, best to shut them down sometime
To process what's visible
And see that what's not

To focus within
The vision inside
Colours what you view outside.

The sights within
Can make you
Break you or shatter you

Shut the window
Let not the world colour
The peace and calm within

Get deeper and swim the depths
Till waters still
Windows then never reveal what's within!

Ideas Brewery

Of kings and queens
Of soldiers and pheasants
Scouring books and stories
Capping the knowledge

The March ahead
Matches conquests
Not the scale I agree
But strife and struggle
Immense indeed

The ideas-a-brewing
Soon release it will
The wait impatient
Time it takes to blossom

Sweet will be the victory
To savour and relish
To enjoy to the hilt
Patience needed indeed!!!

Scaffolding

The support, the safety net
Around a structure
So as to not fall
Something to hold on
In case you slip
A way to step up
And reach your heights

Facilitators, parents and mentors
Take scaffolding to heart
Temporary yet firm
A hand to hold
Step if you miss
To rest and ponder
As you climb
Assistance at a distance
Building your life

Another thought on Scaffolding

I stand caged
Shutters drawn
Grilled and shut
But my thoughts
Climb the scaffolds
That friends hold
Urging pushing
Me to unshackle
Free myself to step up

Path shaky
Bamboos creaky
Rough ties hold joints
A stretch to the next
To be tread with care
Yet go on slow and steady
Those are shoulders strong
Soon you will reach the top!

Interlude!

Cool and chill
The thinking cap on
I think think think
New ideas new goals
New avenues to explore
Time to ponder and wonder
It's me time set asunder
Dressed all chic
And set
To pen down in instant
The brewing bubbling
Thoughts afresh
Keep watching
Waiting wondering
What's it that brims
Under the hat!

Random memories

I remember the butterflies in my stomach
As I got on the stage for the first time

I remember me dressed up as a bride in red,
coy and young

I remember the dark night,
the dark presence
Of something sinister out to harm me

I remember the wait, the anxiety before
Being taken into the operation theatre
For my Caesarian

I remember my best childhood friend's hand
Holding mine and
Nervously pushing the skin
Attached to my nail

I remember the waves washing over me
As I lay on the edge of the expanse of the ocean

I remember the day I walked up to
The college to do something with my life
After giving birth to my sons and
Setting up systems at home to run smoothly

I remember the first day in class
When I had to face children quarter
My age while shivering every muscle

I remember holding dad's soft hands tight
Trying to keep pace with his brisk strides
As he rushed to drop me off at school
Before he left for work

I remember the cool breeze on my face
As I sat upstairs in the double-decker bus
On Mumbai winter mornings
On my way to college

I remember playing char khamba
Aba dhubi, kho kho and khakdi
In the evenings thru my childhood
With my friends in the building

I remember the scooter ride
Riding to the cinema
The movie hardly watched
Hand in hand lost in sweet crime

I remember the heart wrench
Every time my babies leave the nest
To pursue their dreams

Dousing the gas lights

The times she was told about
The slim, energetic fitness
She thought about
Her hormones, Tsujigiri
Her victory residues the weight she carried!

The times she was told about
The agileness, strength and speed
She thanked god
For the battle won
Left with only 20% pain and limp

The times she was told about
Her complaints of heat or the chill
She looked at
Her control over her body swings
But never giving into meltdown binges

The times she was told about
Smart women who achieved
She took pride
The balance of
Upbringing her kids and a sought-after
professional

The times she was told
Health and wealth matter

Anguish

My heart is yet heavy again
I don't know for what
And nor I know why
As my heart is ailing
My Mind is on strike
It does not want to do anything I like

I look within hitting blockheads
I look out and can't wrap my head
What is it? Why is it?
Someone tell me and help me out
All I know is I am hurting a lot

I search for things to happy me
I look for this or that to satiate me
But nothing eggs me on
Nothing fires me up
That is so so unlike me

Oh!! My heart is so so heavy
Is it some hormones going haywire
Or is it something from within the berg
Or is it my illusion that's going berserk
Or is it just plain laziness?

I go round in circles searching, seeking
Looking for answers, all avenues ploughing
Sometimes I blame this; sometimes that
No holiday nor my kids nor anyone close
Is able to fill the void; I am just lost!!!

All I know is I am all alone
Lonely as my soul wanders the deserts lone
Someone to know me, someone to hold me
Someone to hug me; tell me it's fine it's ok
For once someone takes charge of me

I am tired of being strong
Fighting, putting up a brave front
Showing it doesn't matter; it's ok
For others to treat me like a doormat
Hiding my true sensitive emotional self!

Oh stop! Oh stop!

Oh my heart, please calm down
As always find a way to solve
Your problems issues and woes
Rise up and lift your sword
For you still need to fight this battle all alone!!

Creatures of Change

Days dates months, pass
Meaning less they seem
Grains of time, frozen
Yet they trickle by!

Life's churn at the slowest
Restricted and caged
Days designed thus
Etched to teach a lesson

But the tenacious
Resilient and buoyant
Race that we are
Take it on our chin

Memory less days imposed
But twisted into the most memorable
No gathering or meeting
Yet digital gathering the norm

Zoom it, dance it, sing it
Group planks, passing the glass
Each birthday and anniversary
Every event a celebration

Not we the ones to shut down
Locked into our spaces of gloom
Sculpt, paint and create
Music, moves and more

The creativity at its peak
Searching ever for alternatives
Time-warped, never we will
Creatures of change in history!

Something is wrong

A disturbed mind today.
An inexplicable pain .
I know not what
Just trashing about
Struggling to make sense

Never before this chaos
Of heart body and mind
A huge pain cloud
Over my heart

Is it my baby leaving
Is it my beloved
Is it the pressure
Is it some internal changes
Or a grip of depression

I know not
I know not!
I feel distressed and withdrawn
Tears just welling my eyes

Mind rebelling
Legs like jelly
Know not what
Just someone to talk to
To share my deep pondering
Just one to hold my hand

Hug me tight
And say it's alright
No explanation
To my lost strength
To what I feel
I do not know
I truly do not know

Home coming

The wheels speed the track
Time flies past in a crack
The fields the trees the pond
Opens childhood doors abound
Heart racing pulse pacing
Soul shining like the sun
Matching rays smile beaming
Mind churning as wheels run

Eyes search the horizon
Neck stretched out
Seeking the station in vision
Ahhh there it is the slant roof
people porters luggage race by
There stands appa peering
For a glimpse of his beloved child

Time stands still
Nothing has changed
A jump down and a tight hug
The familiar warmth and security envelops
Homecoming of the heart

Tranquil passion

The hues the shades
The orange yellow haze
Setting the sky ablaze
And earth at shadows gaze
Gloriously sets the sun
Setting the waters alight
Peace and calm reign
As hills stand dark and staid
Gently lapping homes in
Birds and boats sailing in
Darkness creeps in softly
the orange glory fades
Serene, tranquil, yet fiery
Balance of mind prevails!

The Stony Sentinel!

They stand like sentinels
Watching centuries go by
Celebrated and etched
Eons ago by crafted hands

The kings in their grandeur
The courtesans in their finery
The Warriors standing tall
Share not they frozen in time

As ages passed, know not
Missed or pleased
With the times that changed
As they stand expressionless

A part of a colossal beauty
An intrigue how mankind managed
The mammoth task
No words out their stony lips

To withstand ravages of war
The fury of weather gods
The damages of time
Tire not they stand ramrod

Oh will they spring alive
Will they sprout tales
Of valor, of squalor, of glory
Of plunder, of abuse

Of will the stand still
Patient, tolerant
Or indifferent
With a heart of stone!!!

Trapped

Oh the shackles of the mind
The love in some things
The crucifying punishment of isolation
Sometimes in sometimes out

Always the wonder
Is it truly love that speaks
Or the position to the world wins
Dread the hot and cold

To live in the same nest
Kept out of ones space
The nearby soul tortured wringing
Wondering if in or thrown out

What use this existence
Not that of love
Caged in the bars
Of society and norms!

Break free an option
Yet self restrictive rules
Positivity of life
Then the biggest enemy to contend!

The Release

Entrapped and encased in
Flesh blood and bones
Twisting and withering
In the fate of being
A fire engulfing, engulfing
The happenings of life present
Waiting to be delivered
Into the arms of the mighty
The release is just a whiff
Snaking out in Nirvana!!

My window to the world!

When the window is large
Laced with sunlit greenery
Neat curtains bordering
A gentle breeze flowing in

Mind feels refreshed
Rejuvenated to think
Churn out fresh
Contemplate afresh

Only window out
Temporary it may sound
But life fresh greens
Keeps the life alive

Constant remains
My window to the world
Silent steady company
To good days and bad

The flow of movement
Birds morning flight route
Busy feet to work
And me watching the world go by

Hold my equilibrium I must
For two quarters more
Fresh verdant and green
Ready to take on the world then.

My Window to the world
My friend and cheer leader
Forcing a smile thru storms
Sustaining the calm in me

The Passage of Time

Different boats sail
Different time frames
Journeys of their own
Trudging steaming sailing

The passage together
The passage alone
Sometimes bright
At times in shadows

All watched by one
Managing the lights
Clustering souls
Destined journeys

All moving in one direction
Some ahead some behind
Charting different paths
Merging would only clash

Sail and sail through
On your own path
Not disturbed by other
Sail through the passage of time

Bookish views!

If I were a book
I would flip
I would scan
I would check
Read the blurb
Of my master

I would discuss
With my friends
On the shelf
Would my master
With ample grey matter
A good reader maketh?

I would pick
I would choose
The author
Best selling one
A master storyteller
To ink my pages

If I were a book
I would adorn
Like a jewel
A book shelf
Of a well read
And not get lost in trash!

Fledgling saga!

The little fledgling takes flight
You bid adieu with a heavy heart
Yet you feel proud too
The lil one is taking its first flight

The lil one with stars in its eyes
Flies to distant lands
With hopes and dreams
A conviction to win the world

Alien lands
Alien people
Alien food
Alien weather

Try try I must , determined
The lil one tries, not letting a peep
Struggling against elements
All new in sight and experience

Initially, a sense of many friends
Over the years many fair weather
Some sailed along
But hardly any stuck through

Fledgling grew wings
But not strong enough
To sail through
The independent troubled flight

It tried solving its issues
Slid down the dark alley
Scrambled up some
All alone the fight continued

Then came a time
It was not worth trying
Better to give in then fight
All belief in self lost

A battle lost
Dreams vanished
Hopes shattered
A sense of failure set in

Wounded , tired and hurt
The lil one returned
The wiser birds realized the peril
Quickly took under their wings

A check for good health and mind
A lot of coaxing and cajoling
Step by step the fledgling grew
In confidence and esteem too

The wise ones held on
Nurtured the lil one
Build up the strength in the wings
Set a path for its flight.

Path not without perils though
The wise one in the wings guiding
And then one day
The young one was ready to fly again!!

The Escape

Captured in time
Within crumbling walls
Behind the red door
Imagining freedom in spirit
Escape mode fixed

Shackled and tied
Self and society abiding rules
The soul seeks release
Fugitive glances to ascertain
Escape unbridled

Yet all in the imagination
Wait for the opportune moment
Writhing emancipated lies
The soul within; desperate
Escape to freedom awaits!!

Crevices

In the cave I lie
Dealing with pain
Licking my wounds
Working towards betterment

The bright flowers , The lush leaves
Invite me out
Peeking in
Through my window to the world

I get tempted occasionally
Gear up, plan the day
Rest well, mentally set
I venture out

The souls around me
Love me so
Make it pleasant
While I assert my independence

Not all forays are pleasant
Million eyes focused on you
Questions, pity , empathy, anger
Contempt , fear all roll by

Places not inviting
For six legged beings
Or the ones on wheels
Well simply not welcome board will suffice

After this onslaught
Back in the cave
Licking the old ones
Then some fresh ones too!

Well think I am safe
In my haven and space
But then invisible eyes pry
Passing judgement on passage of time

Know not they
Every passeth of time
Patience of the soul
Wears off some more

I still lick my wounds
The seen and unseen
But I trust my grit
And wait to rise as a Phoenix !!!

What's Love

I was asked , what's Love
I wonder, i ponder
Is it to die for
Or something to cry for

A feeling? An image?
A passing thought
Shifting its loyalties
In the sands of time?

Love of your life
Baby momma;Child grandma?
Husband wife; friends forever
Changing merging

Is love changing
Is it not eternal?
Me thinks it depends
On the form and kind

Different forms and names
It carries!
Motherly, brotherhood , sisterhood
Platonic, romantic,

Selfless, self love
Obsessive, playful enduring
Yet I wonder any above
Eternal? That lasts for ever?

In the journey of life
Loves come and go
With a purpose you know
Oh ! Does it not make despair

No not really!
Despair surely
When lost you brood
Ecstasy is when you savour and let fly free!!

Nirvana Nirmal

One small little girl
Innocent and naive
Simple wants and needs
Loved and cocooned
All called her Komal Kusum

As she grew
Ponder she did
Of surround and around
Confused and bemused
Masala Madhu came in

Slowly troubles dawned
Tests, exams , frocks
Shoes, umbrellas books
Wants temple
wants
Ganpati Gayu sailed in

Wants were wants
Grew in size
Now cars , house
Gucci, Rohit Bal
Traipsed in Mandir Mandakini

All satiated
Unhappiness set in
Search here there
But in temples
Gossip Gayatri ruled

Saddened and dejected
In a shell she went
Monks saints and sadhus
No solace felt
Trudged Ghayal Gunjan

Slowly it dawned
Neither here nor there
The search had ended
Within herself
She found Nivana Nirmal

Life hues

Shades of blue , pink and crimson hues
Green , brown and yellow varieties too
Just like the shades
Life hands to you

Calming the hues
Visibly Varied appear when serene
The first sign of a ripple
They merge to irrelevance

Shattered the hues
All mixed up and grey
Muddled and confused
As the turbulence hits

Time that heals
Clears life's wounds
Calmness reigns
The shades glitter in individual glory!!

Nostalgia

Gone whoosh
Poyepoche! Vanish!
Those days of innocence
Simple pleasures as a child
Paper boats and kites in the sky
The giggles on the swing
The shout of glee on the slide
Gone forever! Whoosh!

Vanished those days
Of girly gossip and silly banter
Of blind trust and simple faith
Of hero worship and adolescent crushes
Of naive belief in goodness of the world
Of care and comfort of parents homes
Whoosh! Disappeared !
Gone forever!

Gayab! Chole geche!
Those days of first romance
The rose tinted glasses
And the dream of dreamy days
The search for the right mate
Of stars in your eyes
And ambitions to soar high
Vanish ! Gone forever!

Gone too! Vamoosh!
Are the days of struggle
Of burning the midnight oils
The days of diapers and drool
School groups and ptm woes
Of counselling and hawk eyed hovering
Thankfully gone the ferrying kids from one
class to another
Gone gone gone forever

Now the world goes by
Singing it's song
I stand there spent and tired
But Enjoying the buzz around
Savouring my space and solitude
Knowing one day the time will come
This too will, vanish and be gone forever!!!

Friendship

A song? A thought? A feel?
What is it that connects ?
A desire? Some disgust? Or time?
Is that what it is?

A knowing smile! A quick glance
The unspoken word the silence between
These are what make it strong
Beyond and further it takes you along

It's not easy to find one
It breaks your heart to leave one
You learn that for every turn
You need a new one

All types and kinds you get
The lovable, the annoying
The bossy and some snooty
But life with out is never ever complete

On this day of celebration
The sturdy ship sails ashore
The dear ones not of blood
Gather around and become one

The most valued of all
Is the friend always on call
Come rain come shine
Loves you with a curse and a smile

The banter the sauter
The scold the scaffold
The fights the flights
The ever strengthening ties

Life is bland and insipid
With out enough of the stupid
The oasis in the desert
Friendship shines the brightest!

The Juggler

In the middle of the road
Stands he juggling
The balls of life

Trying to catch throw
Balance coordinate
To live his life

In perfect rhythm
He tosses and catches
In control thinks he

A whiff of wind
A distraction maybe
Astray goes one

A step aside
Reels in the wayward
To keep juggling

At times by surprise
Life throws a black one
Offbeat yet juggle

Tune it in
In rhythm with others
The struggle softer

Yellow, white or black
Balls of life
Juggle on with a smile

Mother

She stands tender
in a gentle sway
Harms not a fly
Even with her gaze
The love that pours
Every cell through
Only leads to one in womb
Nurture love with hand
Protecting heavy belly
Every move every kick
hearts a flutter
Silence in the womb
pulse set racing
Fear grips sweating palms
And slowly creeps
Warrior charm

Baby in arms
Eyes hands body
In protective stance
Sentinel mind
In attention stands
Slightest darkness
Shadow falls
Swords drawn
Every cell alive

Attack and kill
No harm befell
Or touch the hair
Of my baby precious!

The Rise and Fall

As you set gloriously
You rise magnanimously
Albeit at two ends

Two ends? Are they ?
You are the same
Standing in your place!

Man can't take the flow
Breaks it he
Just so the confusions blow

Stand you steady
Circles we go
Painting patterns to follow

Day dates years
Times and zones
We divide

Divide divide divide
Just to comprehend
And to manage

Manage? Do we?
While simplifying
Complicate matters

Divide flows
Easy to rule Goes
Boundaries galore

Fight shoot crash
Conquer bounded places
Steadily pulsating you watch

Wondering pondering
Why the confusion
While circumambulating oneself???

Why?

Why am I nice to people?
Why am I kind?
Why do I not change?
Even after being kicked on my face .
Even after being walked over
Even after thought to be an imbecile

I do hurt with harsh words
I do crave for softness from my loved ones I do
expect tenderness
Yet, repeatedly I am pushed
I am shoved
I am spoken to curtly

But then I still want to care
I still want to remain true
I still want to be the kind soft hearted me!
People who shove , push demean
Know their flaw in their hearts
The very reason , they defend up
Coward they are

Can't face their truth
Can't handle the gentle and kind me!
Can't match up to my love
Can't match up to my tenderness
Can't stand up to me!

I do withdraw into my shell
To protect my tender raw heart
But I come out stronger yet
With resolve to face
The unkind world
With a smile on my face

Searching eyes

I wait , eyes beseeching,
On the branch of love
For just one glimpse
Of your enchanting face
Oh my beloved
Oh beloved of mine
I wait for thee
With my heart a flutter!

Letting Go

My heart tore
And wrenched
To leave my son
Albeit a grown man now
To leave him alone
To the uncertainties
We face these lonesome days

But then brace I did
It's his life to live
It's his battles to face
I have the faith in my lil man
To be safe healthy and strong
All by himself
In the tough lonesome virus ridden days

I hugged him
I cried a lil
Filled up his fridge
Then picked my bags
Got into the airport buggy
Waved till I could see
Held my love and faith
To take care and live life well

Burma War

A story about a woman of grit and determination.

The Year 1942
Burma invaded
Japan marches ahead
British retreat, letting subjects
Fight for themselves.

Scores of Indians
Trapped without help
Some walk the long route
Women and children
take to the seas!

Glorious sun sets
Yet on the docks
Gloom spreads
Bereft of their homes
Huddled with possessions bundled.

Sat the refugees
Fleeing from carnage
Bombs, shells, shrapnel
Leaving homes behind
Without looking back.

Alamelu sat huddled
Three young ones bundled
A sewing machine
And all her possession
In a cloth tied!

Ships they awaited
From Rangoon docks
On the last ones a-sail
To the port of Chennai
Their only escape from war!

In the dead of night
Six ships ready to go
Only the old,
Women and children
Allowed to board.

An exodus, people rushing
To secure berth
Long benches lined the decks
Strict vigilance ensured
The police doing rounds.

A woman could carry
Only children two
But Alamelu had three
Strict check ensured
Inching forward she went

The brave mother
Carried a baby in arms
One in hand
And one under her skirts
Terrified children huddled closer!

Once on board
Settled on the benches
Possessions bundled
Sewing machine tucked
And a child under

Ship's horns tooted
Setting sail into high seas
But before the hour passed
Japanese planes dotted
The dark skies approached

Whizz! Boom! Bang!!!
Showered the bombs
Hitting the waters around
Alamelu ducked
Holding her brood closer.

The fireworks lasted
An hour or more it blasted
The helpless passengers
Shrieked cried and wailed
As ships went up in a blaze

Hundreds of eyes
Brimming with tears shone
A mother and three children included
To see the sinking giants
It just could have been them

Four Ship that sailed along
Bombed and sunk down
All in a flash
People who sat beside on the docks
Perish in a blink of an eye.

Bodies shuddering
Fear and grief gripping
Moans and laments
For homes and people lost
Yet thanking their fates proceed.

Alamelu thanked her stars
Sent her gratitude to gods
Survived on the meager food
Sailed the choppy seas
Landed on Chennai shores

Safe yet not aware
Of challenges that lie ahead
Her husband and son
Walking the jungles
Will they land safe back to her?